WHAT, WHY, AND HOW?
-1-

Aslı Kaplan

TUGHRA
BOOKS

New Jersey

Originally published in Turkish as *Ne, Niçin, Nasıl?-1* in 2006.

Published by Tughra Books

345 Clifton Ave., Clifton,

NJ, 07011, USA

www.tughrabooks.com

Library of Congress Cataloging-in-Publication Data Available

Translated by Mustafa Mencütekin

ISBN: 978-1-59784-279-2

Printed by

Çağlayan A.Ş., Izmir - Turkey

Contents

Preface

Let us suppose this universe is a book waiting to be read. Let's flip through its pages together. What do you see? Look to the right, look at the countless beauties displayed to you in the most beautiful and flawless manner. Look to the left, look at the artistry in each blessing and how each is a distinct wonder of creation. Don't close the book just yet...

The universe is a book showing its Maker, the All-Manifesting, the All-Sublime and the All-Wise Maker, and the manifestation of His Divine names and attributes. There are certain aims and wisdom in the creation of all living and non-living beings in this book and our prime obligation as readers are to understand, appreciate and act in conformity with them.

As readers of the book of the universe, we need to first understand that the All-Favoring and All-Bountiful creates all the beauty and art that surrounds us, regardless of whether we are aware or unaware of it. We need to then appreciate the All-Bestowing, Who constantly renews each of these blessings and continues displaying astonishing wonders in each page on the book of the universe with perfect artistry and wisdom.

The book of the universe is there for us to also recognize the Creator and to act in conformity with His wisdom. It is there for us to understand that we live with His will and permission, and to remind us that we will inevitably return to Him and be questioned about what we saw and experienced in this world and about the proofs showcased to us.

What, Why, and How?-1

As the protagonists of this book, we can see that all living entities showcase countless proofs, perfections and wisdom in their creation. There is wisdom in the structure of a tiny particle, the building block of external existence. There is wisdom in the vast universe which has been being created with extraordinary balance and order. There is wisdom in the human body, plants and animals, the mountains and the seas. All of these wonders are the manifestations of the All-Wise and the All-Manifesting.

Our duty as readers, both of this book and the book of the universe, is simple: to recognize and thank the All-Praiseworthy One for all the unconditional beauties and bounties that He has bestowed upon us. Through scientific principles and fascinating facts, this book seeks to remind us of this important duty...

> "God it is Who has made the sea to be of service to you by making it subservient (to His command) so that the ships may run through it by His command, and that you may seek of His bounty, and that (in return) you may give thanks." (Al-Jathiyah, 45:12)

Why don't human beings and animals produce oxygen?

The function of "producing" nutrients and oxygen has been ascribed to green plants and some microorganisms in oceans. They consume the carbon dioxide that is produced by animals and humans via respiration and instead they exhale oxygen to the atmosphere. In this way, the rate of oxygen in the atmosphere is kept balanced. If human beings and animals produced oxygen, the amount of oxygen would increase a lot. And the atmosphere would get an inflammable characteristic. Then, even a smallest spark would start huge fires. Contrary to this situation, if plants continuously produced carbon dioxide like other living beings, the oxygen in the atmosphere would run out rapidly. In a short time, all living beings would die from anoxia.

Which is colder, metal or wood?

Especially in winters, while our body temperature is almost 37 degrees Celsius, room temperature becomes almost 20 degrees Celsius. Certainly, other objects in the room, too, are at room temperature. But, when we touch the objects, we feel the metal parts of the objects colder compared to wooden parts. It is because metal being a good conductor, starts to get heat from us. There happens heat loss in our hand and it feels cold. So, we feel metal as if it was colder. But when we hold the wooden part, because it is the opposite of metal, wood is a weaker conductor so it takes less heat from us. So, we do not feel wood to be much cold as in metal. Actually, metal and wood in our room are at the same temperature. The reason that makes us feel different is only their difference in taking heat from our bodies.

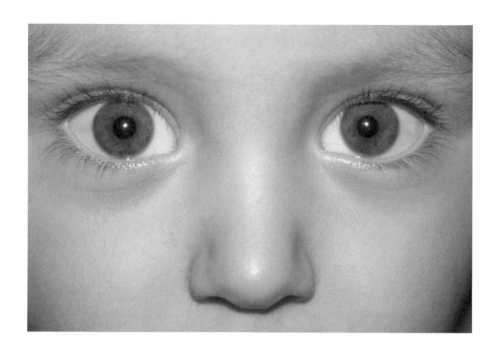

What would happen if we didn't blink our eyes?

Every eye blink virtually washes the eye by spreading tears to all sides of it. Eyelid drags the motes in the upper sides under the lid like windshield wipers of cars. In this way, these motes go away by flood of tears. In every single closing of our eyelids, this salty secretion that comes from our lacrimal glands disinfects our eyes. And this perfect innate system does its duty continually. What would happen if it didn't? If human beings did not blink and eyelids were always open, the cornea that functions as the transportation layer on eyes would dry. Then, it would be covered by another layer that would cause people to become blind.

Why do computer and TV screens buffer before a mobile phone rings?

Mobile phones connect via electromagnetic waves. This electromagnetic energy is mostly felt before the phones rings because information exchange with base station mostly happens at that moment. Monitors and televisions produce display via direction of electrons through magnetic fields. Electromagnetic waves that are spread by mobile phones affect this magnetic field and electrons on it. For this reason, there occurs flipping and skipping on display.

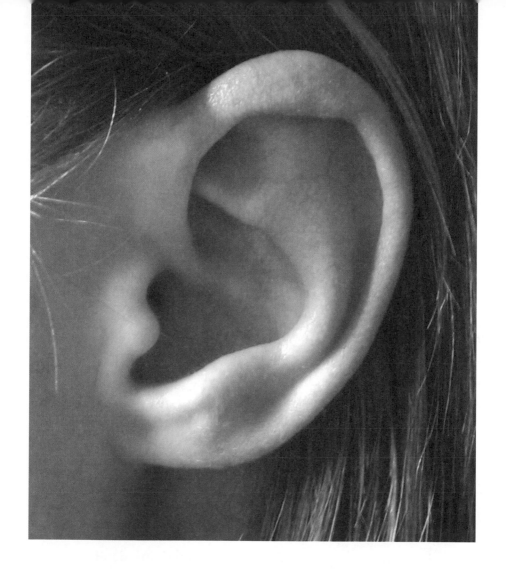

Why do we have two ears?

Ear, one of our five senses, is both a hearing and a balance organ. Thanks to our two ears, which have been given to us by our All-Merciful Creator, we can determine the sounds' directions and how much distance they come from. If we had one ear, our brain wouldn't compare the sounds with each other that come from the surrounding and we wouldn't know exactly where sound comes from.

How does soap clean dirt?

When we wash our oily hands only with water, the oil layer on our skin gives out water immediately. Water does not even wet our hands. And so, cleanliness is not obtained. But using soap changes this situation as one edge of soap molecules is in a hydrophilic character and the other owns a hydrophobic one. That is, one edge of soap molecule wants to touch with water and the other edge does not. In this situation, hydrophobic edge of soap molecules clings to the dirt on our hand; while the hydrophilic edge is released in water. Soap molecules slip by our hand with the pressure of water that we wash our hand. While these molecules slip by, they take the dirt with them which hold on to their hydrophobic edges. The same situation is valid for detergent and dirt while doing our laundry.

What does "seeing mirage" exactly mean?

On a sunny day, you could see small lakes on a warm road and when you try to reach it, you could lose them. Because in reality those small lakes you see is nothing more than the air layer which is close to the road surface. Light hits the warm air layer close to the road surface, is reflected and reaches our eyes. We can also see the objects in the opposite side to us on the reflected surface. This image which is called a "mirage" looks like the reflection of the water surface. So, we assume that there was a puddle on the road.

Do frogs ever rain from the sky?

Sometimes in windy weather, spirals occur that are raised from the ground to the sky. These spirals even take forms of huge tornados. When land tornados are so fast, they can drag cars, humans and animals. Water tornados, if they are in sea, can raise fish, if tornados are in lake or river they can raise frogs and fish, even sometimes mud and small stones into the air. The raising and carrying of things by tornados to the sky fall down to the ground in another area. To express this situation, we often hear sayings such as "… rained from the sky."

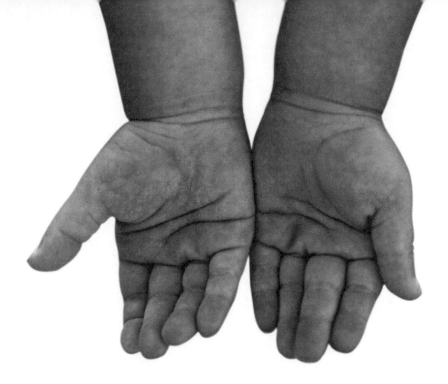

Why do our fingers crack?

When we crack our fingers, the sound does not come from the knocking of bones, as it is commonly thought. Joints of our fingers are limited by joint capsules. These capsules are fully dense and contain pure liquid. When we press our fingers, we enable the split of bones that make up our joints. So, joint capsules are stretched and little gas bubbles inside the liquid that greases the joints blow up. Then, the sound comes which we assume from joints. Overdoing this behavior can cause damage on joint capsules. Also, grasping power can decrease if it is repeated too much.

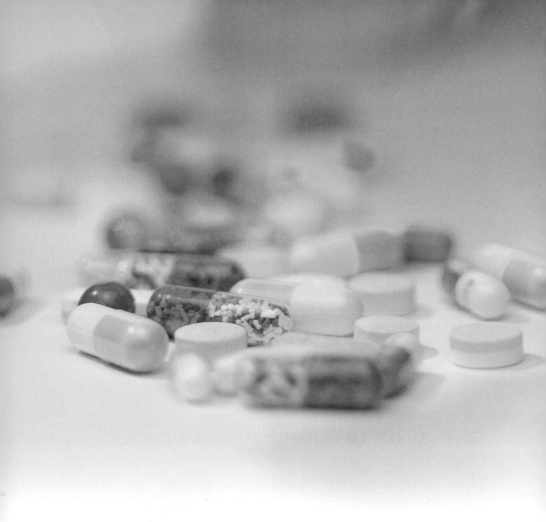

How should we take antibiotics?

Discovery of antibiotics that are used in diseases caused by bacteria has offered huge benefits to humankind. Besides their benefits, these medicines can be quite hazardous in certain situations. The worst hazard caused by antibiotics is the possibility that the particular bacteria shall gain resistance to these agents. War against bacteria that have gained resistance with antibiotics gets harder. This

What, Why, and How?-1

resistance against antibiotics is caused merely by wrong and unnecessary usage. In some situations, the wrong application of antibiotics can even kill beneficial bacteria in our bodies. Of course, this situation immediately spoils the functions of our body. For this reason, the decision of using antibiotics certainly should be made by doctors. The best attitude is simple: not using antibiotics except given by doctors; not taking less or much medicine than it is said by them; and fitting the time of treatment. It also needs to be kept in mind that antibiotics do not work for the diseases caused by viruses. Vital characteristics that are on behalf of human health should not be killed by wrong applications.

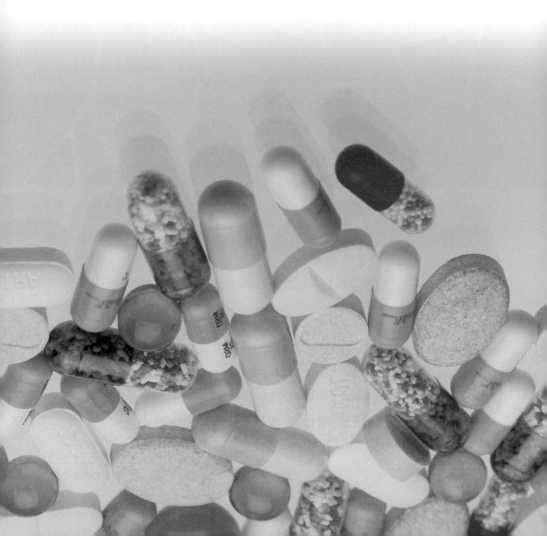

Where does lightning strike most?

Lightning generally strikes to the closest locations to the sky and sharp pointed areas such as antennas, telephone poles, high-tension lines, minarets, trees and sharp rocks. For this reason, it is necessary to stay away from these kinds of sharp points that lightning can possibly strike in rainy weathers. Besides, it is important to take care in not carrying sharp edged umbrellas in that kind of weather. Plus, you should stop standing at the sharpest point around.

What, Why, and How?-1

Why do we sneeze?

Sneezing is the expulsion of air from nose and mouth in a rapid and noisy way as a result of nasal mucosa stimulation. This stimulation can be caused by irritating agents such as pollen, feather, hair, pepper and germs that are accumulated in the respiratory passage. Besides, some other factors can make people sneeze such as light, excitement, shaking and fear. If we pay attention we can easily observe that our eyes are closed while we are sneezing. There is such a big pressure on our head and respiratory system during sneezing that the closure of our eyes becomes a defensive reflex action, which is a sign of the All-Wise, in this situation. The speed of expulsed air from our mouth and nose during sneezing is almost 120 km/h. Sneezing that enables the removal of dust, dirt, pollen or germs from respiratory system should never be held back. Otherwise, a risk of serious damages to our body may rise and that can cause up to a stroke.

What is the difference between fish flesh and the skin from those of other animals?

Apart from the other fleshes, fish flesh contains much more unsaturated fatty acids that are called n-3 and omega-3. Fats that contain much unsaturated fatty acids are of the least risky ones for the health of cardiovascular system. While vegetable oils have more unsaturated fatty acids than animal fats, the healthiest one in animal fats is fish flesh. Fatty acids in fish flesh play a crucial role in children's neural system and brain health. In the case of deficiency of these acids in childhood, even a tendency to depression in the coming ages may be seen. It has also been revealed by scientific studies that consumption of fish plays an essential role in the protection of cardiovascular health in adults. Likewise, the fact that fat acids in fish oil are much more than the amount in the breast milk is indeed good enough to remark the significance of fish flesh. Endowed with such facility for our health and provided for our benefit, this wonderful food should be consumed as much as possible and a particular attention must be paid while it is bought.

What, Why, and How?-1

What is the ozone layer?

Ozone layer is the name of the sphere which is placed in strato-
sphere layer between sixteen and fifty kilometers of atmosphere
and densely contains the ozone substance. Ozone is a gas composed
of three oxygen atoms, and it is colorless at room temperature. It
is showed by the chemical symbol of O3. Ozone layer decreases the
intensity of harmful ultraviolet rays coming from the sun and
blocks their reaching to the earth's surface. High dosages of these
rays cause skin cancer, damage eyes, decrease the growth rate of
plants, and unbalance the ecosystem. In short, it may affect all
beings in the world negatively.

How does a thermos keep the warmth of the materials in it?

There are two pots in a thermos, placed one within the other. The outer pot is metal; the one inside is generally made from glass. The air between these two has been emptied before. In other words, there is an almost perfect emptiness between the two pots generated by manufacturers. There is no conduction of heat due to the lack of air. That is to say, the typical heat exchange cannot take place from outside to inside, or inside to outside. Also, inner and outer surfaces are made shiny to realize the heat insulation in the best possible way. As a result, a thermos in a good quality can preserve the warmth of the things put in it.

Why do rivers and lakes start freezing on the surface?

As water gets colder, it changes form and transforms into ice. When cold increases, this ice layer becomes thicker. Simply because ice is lighter than water, it stays on the water. So, only the top area of the water freezes. In this situation, aquatic living beings under the ice are protected from the cold. As ice hardly conducts heat, the ice layer formed on the upper side does not let cold weather in. So, neither the water in the depths of lakes or rivers freeze, nor living beings in the water. If water didn't get lighter when it froze and if it became heavier like many other substances, the frozen part wouldn't stay on the top. Freezing would start from the bottom and as cold increased it would go upward. There wouldn't be left any living beings in a wholly frozen lake. How nice and happy that such a marvellous characteristic is given to water by the All-Wise and the All-Compassionate.

Why do we sleep?

Just as we cannot survive without water, air and food, sleep is as much a vital need for us. While sleeping, thoughts that make our mind busy, tensions and information we got in the day time are being evaluated one by one. Daily experiences are placed into memory. While our brain cells store enough energy for an entire day, our immune system gets activated. Besides this, growth and regeneration also happen during sleep. So, sufficiency and restfulness are vitally important factors for sleep that covers almost one third of our lives. Daily sleep time changes according to the age and individual differences. For an adult, an average sleep from six to eight hours is enough. But children need more sleep. Otherwise, children cannot benefit from growth hormones sufficiently that are being secreted during sleep. Sleep is a pure blessing and kindness to us.

What, Why, and How?-1

Why does a pressure cooker whistle?

There is steam in a pressure cooker which is generated by cooked foods. With the increasing heat as time goes by, the steam's pressure increases, too. Because the pan lid is closed, this pressure can't leak out. After a certain time, the pressure increases so much that it throws out the lid. It raises the safety valve on the lid and gets out from the specially-made small hole. And while getting out, it makes sounding vibrations. These sounding vibrations are known as cooker's whistle. Through this high pressure occurred in the pressure cooker, boiling temperature of water can increase to more than 100 degrees Celsius. As the temperature of water gets increases, food is cooked faster. In this way, time and money are saved.

How do things stand on the wall by the help of ventouse?

Ventouses are generally made of elastic substances like rubber or plastic and are shaped in the form of a hemisphere. When a ventouse is pressed tightly to a straight surface, the air in the hemisphere is removed. So, there becomes an airless space between the wall and the ventouse. In this situation, the air outside the ventouse makes the pressure only on the outer part of it. And by this way, the staff is held attached to the surface very tightly. So we can hang our things on the ventouse's edge. Putting some air between the surface and the ventouse would be enough to remove it off.

Why is salt scattered on frozen roads?

As the cold increases in winter, snow falls and icings on roads are often observed, especially when temperature declines below zero. Salt is scattered on roads because salt reduces the freezing degree of water. Thereby ice starts melting at the temperature that normally keeps it solid and icing is prevented. If water has not been frozen before salting is done, it doesn't freeze at zero or below zero, after salting. The system of using anti-freeze liquid in car motors functions in the same logic of salting roads. The liquid of anti-freeze unites with water molecules, and prevents water being crystallized and frozen.

Why do our eyes fill with tears while peeling and chopping onions?

There are certain substances in onion; when they come together, they induce tears. These substances are detached from each other by means of the onion's inner skins. But when we chop the onion, they get the chance to come together. Very little sulphuric acid that is released at that time burns our eyes and causes our eyes to fill with tears. To prevent this, we can chop onions under a running tap. The sulphuric acid arising while chopping is sent away by water without burning our eyes. Besides, putting a lemon slice on the cutting board also absorbs the released gas. The structure of this tear inducing gas is totally damaged even by a low heat. For this reason, cooked onion in our foods do not burn and fill our eyes with tears.

Can water be drunk in a non-gravity environment?

In a non-gravity environment, objects stay motionless when they are set free. Although this is the fact, water can be drunk in space which is a non-gravity environment. In other words, water can keep going in astronauts' oesophagus in space because both our eating and drinking will keep going in the oesophagus by spasm movements. Owing to our miraculous creation, water can be drunk even when people lie down.

What kind of hazards does stress cause?

Essentially weakening our immune system, long term chronic stress causes situations that threaten our general health. When immune system gets weaker, the body's resistance to diseases automatically decreases. While the possibility of contraction on upper respiratory infection increases threefold-fivefold times, the risk of heart attack rises more than that. While increasing back and shoulder pains, stress causes fatigue and exhaustion, too. Also, it accelerates aging by damaging the general structure of body.

What would happen if there was no atmospheric pressure?

Air layer that surrounds the earth is called an atmosphere, and it bears a thickness of miles. This protective ceiling, however, applies a rather high gravity upon our bodies. But, none of us gets smashed under this particular gravity called air pressure. After all, keeping our survival would not be possible without this pressure because there is a pressure towards the outside that is realized by the blood in our body that moves really fast. Facts have made it evident that God Almighty has been balancing this blood pressure with the atmosphere's pressure. If such a system had not been created, our all veins would blow up because of high blood pressure.

Why are heater cores placed next to windows?

Windows of our homes are the main heat losing locations, especially if the heat-isolation is not adjusted well. They cause the cold air outside to enter the inside and the warm air inside to go away to the outside. Because of this, heater cores are placed next to windows so that cold air coming through windows to the inside will be warmed a little by their heat emission. And by this method, the heat balance inside the room might be preserved.

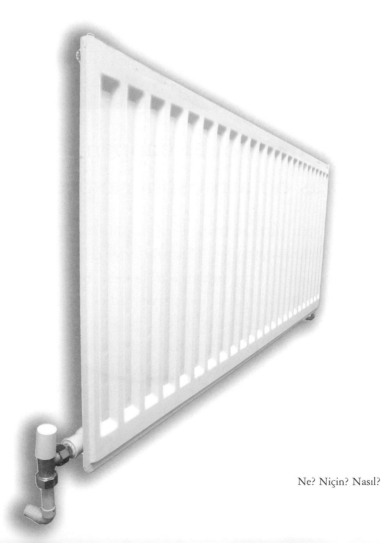

Why do apples get dark short after they are bitten?

There is an acid in apples called tannin. This is also the source of the little sour taste in them. This acid transforms into a brown substance—called as polyphenol—in case of integrating with oxygen in the air. When the apple is bitten, its contact with air starts. The more the bitten part contacts with air, the darker its gets. For this reason, the fruit we start eating should be consumed as soon as possible.

Do fish sleep?

Fish do not have eyelids and they cannot close their eyes as we can. Seeing their eyes always open, we assume that they don't sleep because we close our eyes during sleep. However, this kind of compassion can mislead us. For example, we don't close our ears while sleeping, but when we feel sleepy our brain turns itself off to sounds by the mercy of our Creator. Although our ears are open while sleeping, we don't hear anything because the auditory centre in our brain is turned off. The eyes of fish are open while sleeping just like our ears; but the visual cortex in their brains is set off. So, fish sleep with open eyes, but they do not see anything.

How can flies walk on ceilings?

Tiny suckers have been placed on every single toe of flies. The special liquid secreted from these suckers attaches flies completely to the ground. Through this mechanism, flies can settle on almost every kind of surfaces easily. And they can even walk on ceilings and stay upside down.

What is a barcode?

A barcode is a kind of label that is put on many products. Generally, it is shaped in a rectangular form. It consists of thin and thick black lines drawn parallel to each other, and spaces between these lines. Lines include only the reference number of the particular product. The price of the product and other information about the product are stored in the computer that "reads" the barcode. Computer sends the price of a product to the cash register after "reading" the barcode number. Through this, prices of products are lined rapidly. If barcodes included price information of products instead of reference numbers, barcodes would need to be changed in every price change. This situation would lead to a huge loss in terms of cost and time. In the current system, since price information of products is stored in computers, changing price information in computers is enough for updating. Barcodes also enable to assess the number of remaining products on shelves.

Why do corns become white when they are popped?

When a corn kernel is heated, water in it transforms into steam and generates a particular type of pressure. This pressure pops corn when it starts to force its husk. When this process takes place, the fluffy whiteness coming out is actually nothing but the starch in the corn kernel.

Where in Turkey does cooking take the longest time?

The place where the longest time needed for cooking in Turkey is the highest hill of this country: Mount Ararat (Ağrı). And that is the Mount Everest of the world. This is simply because water doesn't boil at 100 degrees Celsius at high altitudes as it typically does at sea level. As going up the high altitudes, the boiling degree of water gradually falls down because of decreasing pressure. To start boiling, a liquid's own inner pressure and the air pressure of the environment must become equal to each other. At high altitudes, the inner pressure of boiling water's equalization to outer pressure takes place earlier than it does at sea level. And at that time, water starts to boil at the temperature lower than 100 degrees Celsius. So, the food in the water with a lower boiling temperature is cooked later than the one that is cooked in the water that boils at a higher temperature.

How do pens work?

There is a metal ball on the tip of the pen that we can see easily if we look closer. This metal ball can roll everywhere without moving off. Through this rolling system, as one side of the ball touches the paper, the back side touches the ink. When we move the pen on the paper, metal ball rolls and the side which has touched to ink before starts touching the paper this time. By repetition of these movements, writing is realized.

How do raindrops fall to the ground, vertically or diagonally?

Even though sometimes we assume raindrops falls diagonally, rain drops in fact come down from the sky in a vertical style. We can especially be mistaken easily while travelling in a vehicle, since we assume that rain drops move due to the speed of our car. Indeed, though rain drops occasionally fall diagonally by the effect of wind, they always fall vertically.

Why do we see ourselves upside-down on a spoon?

Spoons that are made from shiny metal act as a mirror. But, the inner surface of a spoon reflects our image as a concave mirror and the outer surface reflects us as a convex mirror. As we know, images on concave mirrors are seen upside-down and on convex mirrors, straight. For this reason, we see ourselves upside-down when we look inside the spoon, and straight when we look outside.

Which is better, a bar of soap or liquid soap?

If soaps are shaped in bars, they are consumed by many people, many times. Of course, every single user leaves several microorganisms on the soap. These microorganisms like humid or static environments because they can easily multiply there. Then, the soap that is used for cleaning becomes a good habitat for germs. For this reason, if you have to use a bar of soap, small ones should be preferred. Besides, soap should be washed after every use and it should be left clean. But, things are rather different for liquid soaps. Only the amount of soap that is taken to hand from liquid soap's bottle is used. The soap user doesn't have any contact with the soap remaining in the bottle. Moreover, liquid soap is much more economic by reason since it is not wasted away like a bar of soap as it stands by itself.

Why does milk boil over?

Most milk consists of water. There are a little fat, protein, lactose and similar minerals in the milk, apart from the water. Fat globules in milk rise up when they get warmer and make a bark over the hot milk. Steam bubbles originating in hot milk are prevented by this bark when they go up. The number of these steam bubbles increases in time. And at a certain time, these united bubbles reach enough pressure power that it can tear the bark formed on the milk. It is this moment milk boils over. As stirring milk prevents the formation of fat bark over the milk, milk doesn't boil over when it is stirred continuously until boiling.

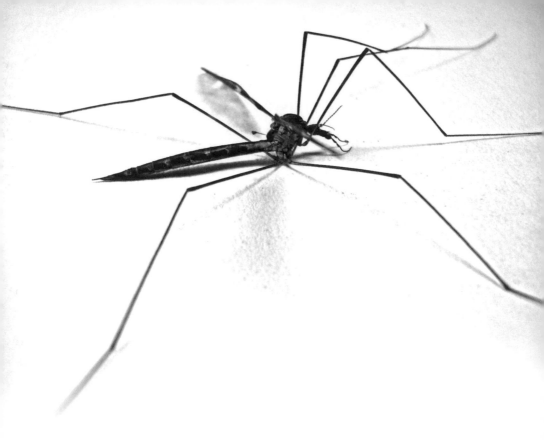

Why do flies appear in summer?

Flies that have been created very sensitive to temperature changes can only live in warm habitats. They are affected by heat decline even if it is a minor decline when clouds come in front of the sun. For this reason flies can't live in winter days. They disappear with the start of cold days. But, they bury their eggs into soil before dying or leave them to other suitable places. Eggs and larva are not affected by the cold. They stay alive where they are left until weather gets warm again. When summer heat comes back, eggs are cracked and after a short time flies start to fly around again.

What, Why, and How?-1

How much water should we drink?

We lose almost three litres water for many reasons during the day. This water loss is caused not only by sweat. Our body loses water even by breathing. And this lost water must be replaced somehow. Sometimes even if we try to meet this with other kinds of food and drink, the best substance is always water for soothing our thirst. Adults owning healthy bodies and normally functioning kidneys and livers ought to drink almost three litres (eight–ten glasses) of water a day. Of course the amount of need can change according to the individual ages and people. Especially, drinking water in the morning as soon as one wakes up, is when the stomach is almost empty, which purifies the whole organism from toxic materials. Besides, it provides people to be more energetic and alert. In summer months, as body loses water by heat and sweat, more water should be consumed than the usual amount. In that way, body temperature could be balanced and moisture on the skin could be preserved.

Why do ice cubes stick together when they are thrown into a glass?

When we put a piece of ice to a glass full of water, ice cube starts to melt by means of the heat taken from the point it touches the glass. As the second ice cube we put into the glass touches the first one, these ice cubes stick together immediately. It is simply because the ice cube, whose temperature is below zero, freezes the ice cube which has already started melting at the place it touches. If one or two drops of water fall to the ice cube whose temperature is below 0 °C, it freezes immediately on ice. We experience the same when we take ice cubes in our hands. Because the moisture on our skin freezes with the coldness of ice cube, the ice cubes we touch stick to our hand. Due to the same principle, we have to be careful when touching metal surfaces as well. For example, if you hold a piece of iron in a cold winter day, you can not pull your hands off easily as the moisture on your skin freezes immediately by the coldness of the iron.

40. Do we really need to sunbathe?

In summer, more ultraviolet rays reach the Earth by sun light compared to the other seasons. Our skin has been created in a condition that can protect itself when it stays under the sun for a certain time. When it is exposed to more rays, it gets bronze. In fact, bronze skin is an alarm that the body has absorbed ultraviolet rays. After a few periods of tanning, the protecting effect of tanning is lost. Then, drying and cracks take place on the skin. And this accelerates the aging process of skin by time. For this reason, it is recommended not to walk outside between 10.00 a.m. and 4.00 p.m. when ultraviolet rays are dense.

How does a tornado take place?

Tornados are whirl-shaped strong winds that occur by sudden pressure change in a narrow field. The cause of sudden pressure change in the atmosphere ascends warm air very quickly. In case that a cold air mass goes up to a warm air mass, the warm air with lower density rises into the cold air very quickly. At this moment, the pressure decreases rapidly. This sudden change in pressure and temperature makes strong winds develop in a very short time. As air continues to rise, the speed of wind increases more and more and finally turns to a strong whirl. Then, it rises up turning in the

42

form of a cone. As rapidly raising air in the whirl quickly gets colder, the water steam inside intensifies. This makes air mass the centre of which turns to a grayish white be seen as a tornado. As long as condensation exists, the extending edge of the tornado reaches down to the ground. Horizontal winds inside the tornados that reach up to a speed of hundreds of kilometers per hour can destroy cars, trees and even houses. Vertical streams on the other hand, blow away the destroyed objects. Tornados mostly take place at plain and tropical locations that open to oceans. However, it may still happen at very plain locations and situations when the pressure changes between air layers happen all of a sudden.

Why doesn't the loud sound
of cicada deafen itself?

The loudness level of a cicada's sound is equal to the one generated by the explosion of a grenade. Interestingly, the cicada doesn't get deafened by the sound that it generates itself simply because the hearing organ of the insect has been protected. The organ has surprisingly been put in a special capsule far from its abdomen.

What, Why, and How?-1

Why is one side of an egg round and the other side is pointy?

If eggs were cornered, their edges would be very weak and could easily be cracked. If they were shaped in the form of a sphere— which is indeed the most enduring geometrical form—it would continuously roll until it hit an object. In both cases, they would either be simply lost or cracked. However, eggs in their current shape do not advance straight forward when they are rolled. They fallow a circular destination on the thin side, and stop at a point close to where they have started to roll. Besides, they are resistant to crack easily.

How can we say "stop" to tooth decays?

Sugar is the most liked food for the bacteria inside our mouths. Bacteria eat the remaining of sugary food on our teeth and turn them into acid. And these acids attack our teeth and corrode them a little, at every turn. In the course of time, small black holes come into existence on our teeth. Then, these holes get bigger and bigger, and turn into decays by continuous acid attacks. However, it does not mean that we should never eat sugary food to protect our teeth from calories. Generally, desserts that are eaten between meal times damage teeth more than those eaten at meals as nibbling little by little along the day provides a suitable position for bacteria to produce acid on teeth. For this reason—besides brushing our teeth after meals—washing our mouths off with water after nibbling helps a lot because bacteria start to produce acid causing decay twenty minutes after eating something.

What, Why, and How?-1

What is the difference between reason and intelligence?

Reason is the ability of distinguishing right from wrong, making an opinion and generating ideas about any topic. As a human being matures, his/her reason develops. Intelligence, on the other hand, provides understanding, comprehending, judging and solving an event with an explanation. In general, the development of intelligence is rapid until twelve, continues up to the age of twenty and then becomes steady after all. Intelligence may not provide people with the same level of skills, in front of all kinds of events. For example, a good poet may not be able to solve a simple mathematical problem, as intelligence differs according to mental events, ability of perception and memory, interests and inclination.

Why does water get warm late and get cold late?

The evaporation and freezing speed of water is very low. So, water can protect its recent temperature for a certain time at moments of sudden warming and cooling. This particular creation acts as an essential role in that our Earth protects its temperature the larger part of which is covered by water. In this way, as the water in the areas that get plenty of sun during the daytime becomes warm late, the Earth's surface doesn't experience a sudden and high change in temperature. In the parts which live night at that time at the same period, the water that has become warm during the day time and not cooled yet, functions almost as a kind of central heating. And all these extraordinary events protect the Earth's surface from sudden cooling. Thus, temperature difference on the Earth's surface between night and day stays at a certain limit that living beings can always endure. If the proportion of water on Earth was less than land, the temperature difference between night and day would increase much. And that would make the life of living beings unbearable and even impossible.

What, Why, and How?-1

How do pearls originate?

When dust, sand, pebble and harmful parasites go inside of mussels and oysters, these living beings get disturbed from this situation. To protect themselves from these foreign substances, they start to secrete a special substance from the protector layer that covers their internal organs. This special secretion of defense system that has been given to them by God is called "nacre." And then, they cover the outer surface of foreign substance that had come in with this nacre. When covering is complete, it means a piece of pearl has originated. In time, pearl gets bigger and bigger by added layers of nacre, layers after layers.

How much milk should we drink?

Milk causes iron deficiency for children if they drink it more than half a liter per day. And this deficiency affects brain development and learning negatively. It also causes anemia and tooth decays. Plus, drinking milk constantly and more than the average amount brings about malnutrition. For this reason, the best is to keep a balanced and broad-array diet, rather than a single line.

Can watermelon be cooled under sun?

The best way of cooling watermelon at a picnic is cutting the melon into two and putting it under the sun simply because the water drops on the surface of the melon take heat from the watermelon in order to evaporate. In this way, the melon loses some of its current heat and becomes cooler in the same way that the cologne we put on our hands refreshes us while evaporating. If we keep leaving the watermelon under the sun although the water drops on it have evaporated, the watermelon shall start getting warmer again.

Why do glasses crack?

When warm water is put in, the inner surface of a cold glass contacting with heat dilates immediately. In the mean time, the outer surface of the glass which remains cold and cannot find the time to dilate is pushed by the warmer inner side. And then, the glass cracks. The same happens when cold water is put into a warm glass.

Why do some buildings
have a swing door?

Generally swing doors are preferred by hotels and similar big buildings because these buildings always need to be kept warm. Cold air goes inside easily through normal doors that are opened and closed all the time. In this situation, the heating systems of these big buildings shall restart every time it gets cooler inside. And that simply means extra consumption of energy. Swing doors prevent the warm air inside to go outside and vice versa. In this way, the necessary saving of energy is done.

Why doesn't honey get spoilt even though it is kept outside?

The reason why food gets spoilt is the fact that organisms such as fungus and bacteria cause rotting, molding and deterioration. However, like all other living beings, these organisms, too, need water to stay alive. Interestingly, honey is a substance that doesn't contain as much water as living beings need to survive. For this reason, honey is a particular habitat where organisms causing decomposition cannot live.

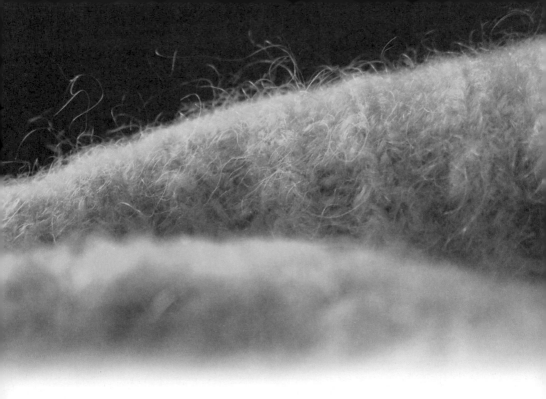

Do woolens really warm people up?

We wear woolen clothes in cold days so that we do not feel cold. In fact, woolen clothes don't warm our body; they just prevent our body temperature from escaping outside and keep the cold air away. That is, wool is not a heater, but an insulator.

How do airbags operate?

There are some chemicals inside airbags such as sodium azide and iron(III) oxide (or ferric oxide). In the moment of a car crash, these chemicals join together very quickly with a sudden spark. As a result of this joining, the gas of nitrogen ignites. When the gas of nitrogen fills the airbag, the bag gets swollen. Indeed, all these happen only in eighty four millisecond, namely in a moment.

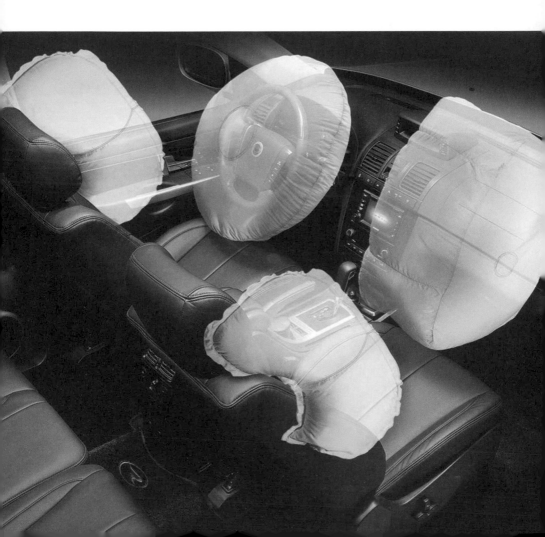

How do some chewing gums and candies refresh our mouth?

The evaporating temperature of aromas inside the mouth refreshing chewing gums and candies is very low. So, they easily evaporate on the heat in our mouth. While they are evaporating they take heat from our mouth. We feel freshness and spaciousness because of the heat transfer from our mouth to the candy or chewing gum.

Why have cats been created with whiskers?

The roots of a cat's whiskers are particularly placed in the parts of the body where nerves and veins are condensed. Cats feel even the little changes in the airflow by means of their sensitive whiskers. As they feel the flow of air around the objects, they don't hit here and there. Besides, whiskers function as a ruler and help cats deciding whether they can pass through a hole or not.

Why doesn't the thin filament in the bulb melt?

The twisted and thin filament used in bulbs is made from tungsten metal. The most significant reason for preferring this metal is its very high melting and boiling point which is 3410 degrees Celsius and 5900 degrees Celsius. During lighting, the heat inside the bulb doesn't increase that much and the filament doesn't melt. The other reason why the filament does not melt is the gases of argon and nitrogen inside the bulb. These gases function in taking heat away from the glowing filament.

How does a broken bone recover?

Even though bones have a very hard structure, they can get broken when they are exposed to a strong stroke. Doctors restore the direction of a broken bone and put it in a cast. At this time, the self-fixing mechanism created in bones starts functioning immediately. Firstly, the blood around the broken bone gets clotted. Indeed, this is a very big clot. Then, this huge clot turns into a tough bone by means of minerals secreted from the bone-generating cells. And after a certain time, the broken bone becomes safe and sound like before.

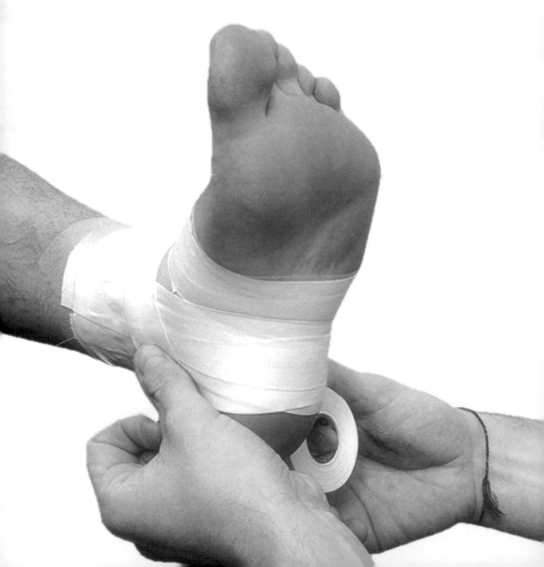

What does "non-freezing animals" mean?

There are particular chemical substances in the blood of some animals which function like anti-freeze in car radiators. These special substances are created in such a special way that they get attached ice crystals in the blood of those animals in order to prevent those crystals from multiplication and unification. So, these animals can survive easily in extremely cold habitats without freezing. Interesting enough, some of those animals have been observed to live unhurt in an ice cap for three years.

How does rain turn into snow?

Clouds are originated by condensation of the water steam that rises from the earth to the sky, by God's absolute Knowledge, Command, Power and Will. If these water drops forming clouds meet with cold air, they turn into thin ice pieces. And then, they fall to the ground by coming together. So, water drops in clouds turn directly into snow by the effect of extreme cold air, skipping the phase of rain.

How do microwave ovens operate?

Microwaves that provide heating in ovens consist of electromagnetic waves. These waves affect food molecules directly. Through crashes between molecules in motion, food gets warm in a very short time and is cooked in a moment. But, in electric ovens as the water or oil of the food absorb the heat, cooking takes place longer. Instead of metal dishes, glass or plastic dishes should be preferred in microwave ovens as microwaves can't pass through metals. Also, since microwaves are very dangerous for the human body, we must take care of not letting them leak out of the oven.

How does water extinguish fire?

Firstly, when water is poured on a burning object, it takes heat from it. Then, the water evaporates by the heat taken. This steam surrounds the burning objects and hinders the oxygen reaching the burning object. Of course, without oxygen nothing can burn.

What, Why, and How?-1

Why do puffer fish swell?

Puffer fish are very slow swimmers so that's why they have been created in a form that they can protect themselves by swelling as they are unable to escape from enemies. They swell by sucking up sea water and double their size in this way. And at this time, thorns covering its skin steepen, too. Since it will be very hard to eat a swollen and thorny fish, its enemies give up attacking.

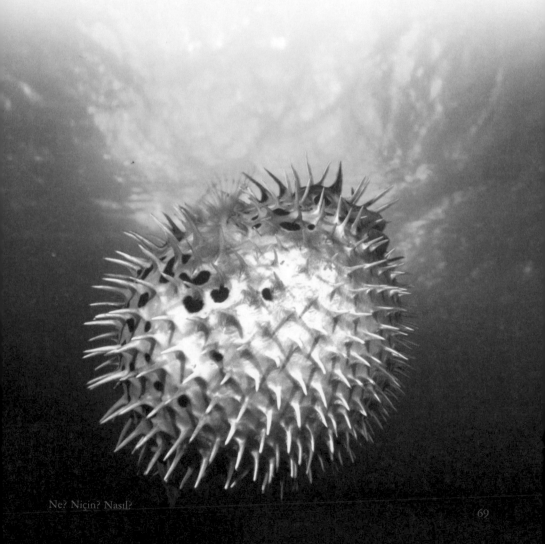

Why does paper make a sound while it is being torn?

Paper consists of cellulose fibers. When we tear a piece of paper, these fibers separate from each other. The vibration that fibers make while detaching causes the occurrence of sound waves in the air around. The faster we tear the paper, the more sound comes as we tear more fibers off in a certain time.

Why can't we tickle ourselves?

When a person is tickled, little nerve fibers on the skin immediately begin to act and send signals to the brain. At this time, as the alertness of the brain increases, pulse and heart beat increase, too. However, our brain was created in a particular form that can distinguish which alerts come from ourselves and which come from outside. And it gives priority to reactions which come from outside. For example, accidents like burning our hand are the situations that need urgent reflex. Therefore, when we are tickled by someone, we react. But, when we try to tickle ourselves, our brain decreases sensitivity at these points and we don't get tickled.

Is it possible to find the age of trees?

When a part of a tree trunk is taken and examined, rings are seen on it, one inside the other. Rings line up starting from the bark of the tree towards the inside. Every one of these rings shows the year that the tree lived. So, we can understand how many years the tree lived by means of counting all of the rings. The spaces between the rings define the capacity of wood that the tree produces in a year. Consequently, the wideness of these spaces can give information about the season conditions that the tree has experienced. If spaces are narrow it means that that particular year passed in drought; if they are wide it means that year was wet.

What, Why, and How?-1

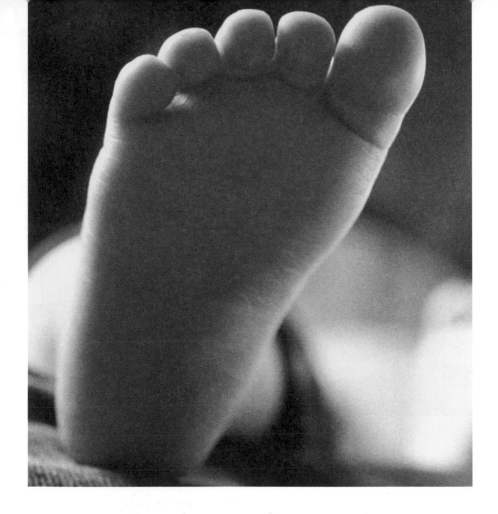

Why do our feet tingle?

When we sit cross-legged by placing our leg under us or in similar forms, veins in our legs can tighten. In this situation, the flow of blood in our veins is somewhat prevented. When the pressure is removed, we feel stings at the edge of our legs till the blood flow is balanced. This situation, that makes us feel as if thousands of ants were walking on our feet, is called a tingle.

Why is lying on a hammock comfortable?

There is a pressure on every object according to its weight and surface that it touches. The wider area the weight of an object spreads the less pressure the object applies on the surface. As we lay on a soft bed or hammock we feel comfortable because every single part of our body contacts with the ground and our weight spreads to a wide area. On the contrary, the reason why we feel uncomfortable on a harsh stool is due to the fact that our weight is spread on the small area of the stool. In this situation, the pressure on us is rather more. The same is true for why women have difficulty with walking on high-heeled shoes.

What, Why, and How?-1

Why can't we tear a newspaper in width smoothly?

We can easily tear newsprint smoothly from top to down, but when we try to tear the same page in width, there definitely emerges some zigzags. This is simply because of the fact that wood fibers—the main substance of newspapers—is lined up on the newsprint from top to down. For this reason, the perpendicular tear we have made on the newspaper goes down smoothly, pursuing the track of fibers. But while tearing a newspaper in width, the tear makes a zigzag every time it meets a fiber.

Why do our hands and feet wrinkle when they stay in water too much?

Almost every inch of our body is covered with hairs. We can see some of them easily, but we can notice most of them only by looking carefully. Sebaceous glands have been placed in the bottom of these hairs. The fat that these glands secrete generates a waterproof layer at the particular area. So, as penetration of water inside our skin is prevented, our skin is kept soft. However, since there is no hair on our fingertips, palm and sole, there is no protective fat layer on those parts. Besides, these areas are covered with a thick skin layer. Because of these facts, when our hands and feet stay in water for a certain time, water penetrates under our skin and tries to find a place for itself. At the end, the thicker skin on these parts dilates and wrinkles because there is not enough area for that water.

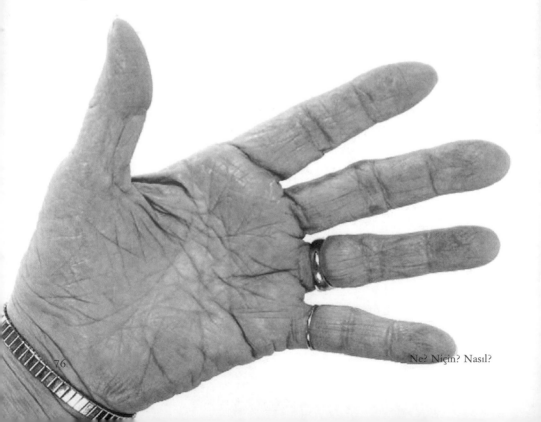

Why do fish-eating birds sometimes stand on one leg?

The legs of some birds such as storks, flamingos and herons are rather bony that they do not have fatty substances to insulate heat. Therefore, their legs get cold very quickly. Sometimes they stand on one leg and pull the other leg on their body in order to warm it among their feathers.

Why do we feel tired after meals?

To supply the necessary energy for digestion, a big amount of blood in the body rushes to our stomach area whenever we eat our meals. This operation decreases the amount of the blood at a critical level that goes to the other parts of our body. As our muscles need oxygen and nourishment transported by blood, a general weariness and inertness are felt in our body.

What does "being crippled by the bends" mean?

Air pressure is 1 atmosphere at the sea level and respiratory and circulatory system of human body has been adjusted to this pressure. However, when people dive deep in the water, the level of air pressure on the human body increases 1 atmosphere every 10 meters. Namely, the closer one dives to the bottom, the more pressure water applies to the body. During this process, gases such as oxygen and nitrogen in the air taken from the aqualung, spread to the tissues by dissolving in blood. While moving up from the bottom to the surface, these gases dilate quickly with the decrease of pressure, in case one rises up very fast. Oxygen does not cause any problem since it is used in tissues. However, when nitrogen dilates in veins suddenly, embolism, lung laceration and even paralysis can happen. Incidents can even end up with death. For this reason, in order to get rid of crippling by the bends, moving up from bottom to surface should be done slowly, and people who have dived should wait at certain depths for a certain time before reaching the surface.

Do male mosquitoes have proboscis?

Proboscises are the organs of mosquitoes that they use for sucking blood. However, because only female mosquitoes suck blood, only they have proboscis. Female mosquitoes carry their eggs inside them. Protein is necessary for the growth and development of these eggs. Blood is a good source for this protein. So, female mosquitoes provide the protein needed for their eggs by sucking blood. Male mosquitoes have not been created for having eggs and raising them by storing blood, so they don't have proboscises. That is to say, the blood that is taken from other living beings by mosquitoes is only for eggs, not to feed themselves. Saps are indeed the mere source of nourishment for mosquitoes.

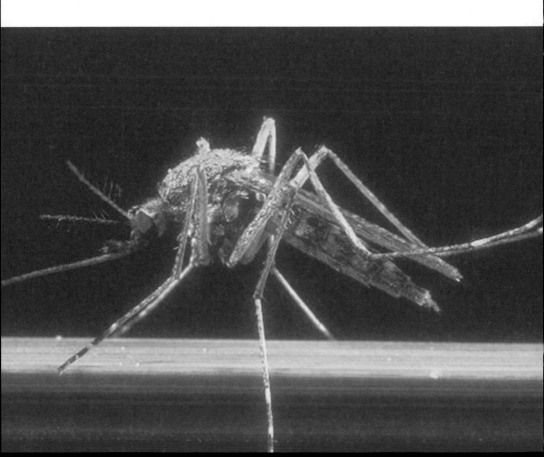

What is tanning?

Tanning, so that the color of our skin changes under the sun, is actually the title of the chemical reaction that the color cells in the derma layer on our skin experiences. These cells immediately increase the amount of dark color substances called melanin when they are exposed to ultraviolet rays in the sunlight. Therefore, the color of our skin gets darker under the sun. Actually, the reason for this darkening is to protect our skin from the effects of ultraviolet rays, because melanin sucks ultraviolet rays. But, if someone keeps staying under the sunlight, this protecting process doesn't get along. Even though the color of our skin darkens, namely it is covered by melanin, some parts of ultraviolet rays continue to penetrate our skin. In the end, excessive exposure to ultraviolet rays eventually can even cause skin cancer. Every year, half a million people suffer from this disease, and the rate of it especially increases among young people.

How do our nails get longer?

Hand and foot nails come from their roots under the skin that are very close to the bottom of the nails. At this part nails become very thin and get the shape of a half-moon in white color. This part is most evident on thumbs. The cells at root produce keratin, a dead kind of cell. As new organic cells come up, dead nail is pushed outside. For this reason, as it happens with our hairs, we don't feel pain while cutting our nails.

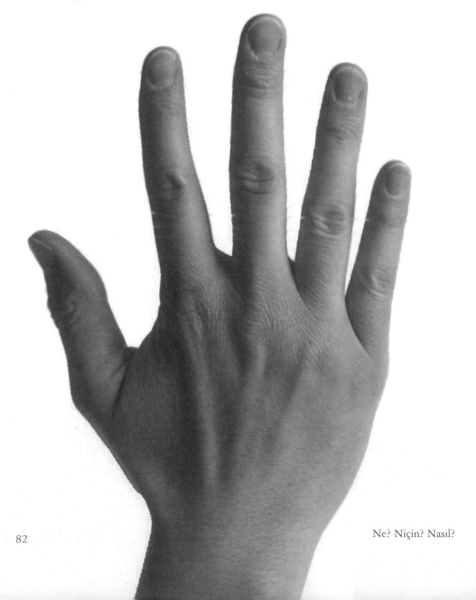

Why do the bones of old people break more easily?

The strength of bones has been provided by calcium and phosphate minerals. The crystals that are combined by these minerals are present only in a single part of the bones of young people. Growing older, crystals spread all over the bones. And at that time, bones lose their qualification of elasticity at a high degree. This situation makes bones break easily and be restored in a longer time after they are broken.

How do phones operate when power is cut?

There are basically two cables in two colors connecting our phones to the socket on the wall, and from there to the operation center. One of these cables is the common talking line. The voltage level of the current coming from the centre to our phone via the other cable is between six and twelve volts. For this reason, even though the power is cut at home, our hard line phones continue to work because necessary power is provided from the operation centre. In case the power of the centre is cut off, too, the battery system in the centre is automatically operated.

Are there any planets out of the Solar System?

Like the planets revolving around our star, the Sun, there are other planet systems revolving around other stars. According to the data of the year 2003, it has been proven that there are 107 planets around 93 stars out of the Solar System. Still there exist some other planets, but their existence has not yet been officially approved. All of those discovered planets are at least 30 times bigger than the Earth. However, this dimension difference is not because all planets are very big. Rather, our observation tools can only observe the big planets for the time being. The last-discovered planet looks like our Earth. According to the declaration made by NASA on June 13th 2005, the last-discovered planet is fifteen light-years far from the Earth. It revolves around a star named Gliese 876, and its orbit is very close to its star. Its diameter is twice the size of the Earth, and its mass is approximately six times heavier than the mass of the Earth.

How do horses sleep while standing?

Horses have been created in a nature that they are able to lock their knees while standing. Thanks to this feature, they can stand a very long time without lying on the ground; they can even sleep while standing. Researches present that horses feel more comfortable sleeping in this way since they consume less energy while standing. As the body of a horse is rather big, its internal organs can make the horse breathe in difficulty while lying down.

Why do clouds get gray before rain?

Since clouds reflect the light, they are mostly seen in white color. Before rain, water drops in the cloud get bigger and the reflection rate of the cloud decreases. This time, rather than reflecting, the cloud starts to absorb the coming light. Due to this process, we start to see that cloud in gray.

Why does our hair become white in time?

Every single hair is like a tube with the middle of which is empty. There are color substances called melanin in the cavity of that middle part. At young ages, there is a liquid that holds the melanin—that gives the hair its color—together in that cavity. But, as people grow older, this liquid is gradually lost because the skin comes in a situation that can't produce the hair as healthy as before. Since colorific cells can't find an environment to hold on, they stay up in the air. Therefore, hair loses its color and turns to white.

How does our nose smell?

The concept we call smell is actually evaporating chemical particles from objects, namely volatile smell molecules. In every single
breath we take, air enters through our nose to the inside of our
body. Special bones in our nose direct some part of air to the smell
sensor area in the upper part of the nasal cavity. Therefore, smell
molecules that enter through our nose reach that particular section
to be defined by the air we take while breathing. We take all kinds
of smell during inhaling and exhaling.

How is dry-cleaning done?

The substance that dissolves the dirt on our clothes in both the washing machine and hand washing is the detergent and water. In dry-cleaning, however, a petroleum product called perchloroethylene is used. In other words, cleaning is not done in a dry environment in dry-cleaning. Clothes are washed not with water but with another solvent.

What, Why, and How?-1

How do hurricanes occur?

Hurricanes occur when cold air currents come on warm oceans. The cold air rises up after taking some of the heat from the ocean and then generates a low air pressure area. Then, the high pressure air around starts rushing into the low-pressure area, being under the command of the All-Mighty. Next, the air current misses the low-pressure area and rushes to the next area; then it starts to revolve around the low pressured area. And this is called a hurricane.

Is there any fish that can survive without water?

Almost all fish die in a short time when they stay out of water. However, there are some kinds of fish who have a lung which can live without water for a few months in streams and rivers of Africa. In the hottest days of summer, water in Africa dries for a few months. When water ebbs, these fish with lungs bury themselves into the mud of streams. And they properly cover their surrounding with mud. They leave a small hole opening to the air for breathing. Therefore, they live for a few months by using their lungs until the stream is filled with water again.

How hot is the Sun?

The surface temperature of the Sun which is a little bigger than the average big star is approximately 6000 degrees Celsius, and its inner temperature is 20 million degrees Celsius. As some stars with a size of one tenth of our Sun might be seen in outer space, there are 100 times bigger stars than the Sun. While the surface temperature of stars which are less dim than the Sun is about 3000 degrees Celsius, that of those similar to the Sun is about 6000 degrees Celsius, and that of the bigger ones is 30000 degrees Celsius and higher. The stars with a very high heat have huge masses, as well.

Why are the birds perching on wires "not" shocked?

Electricity is an energy that is conducted by the way that electrons hit the adjacent atoms and vibrate them. The electric current that goes out from a generator through one of the two wires in the cable, comes back from another neutral wire after turning on the lamp. The electric current never chooses the resistant way, but always prefers the shortest and simplest route to reach the soil. The birds on the electric wires don't have a connection with the soil. That is, they don't serve as a short way for electricity to go to the soil. The electric current prefers the wire between the two legs of birds, instead of passing through their bodies because the wire presents less resistance to the current than the bodies of the birds. For this reason, birds can settle a day long on bare electricity wires conducting high voltage. However, if a bird accidentally contacts with the pole that holds electricity wires, the body of that bird becomes the shortest way to go to the soil for the current. Electric current shall pass to the soil via the body of the bird and pole, and then the bird dies this time.

What, Why, and How?-1

How does ice swim on water?

Water is the only created substance in nature where the volume of which increases and the density of which decreases when it freezes. This solid and frozen form of water is called ice. Namely, the density of ice is lower than that of the water. For this reason, ice can swim on water. If this specialty hadn't been ascribed to water, the ice coming up at times when water freezes on seas, lakes and streams would sink down to the bottom. And as a result of this, all of the living beings in the water would die.

Could the Earth be
created smaller?

A smaller Earth would have had a weaker gravity. And, the gases surrounding the Earth and composing the atmosphere would leak out to space. Of course, there would be no life on an Earth lacking atmosphere. If the Earth were bigger than today's size, the gravitational power would increase too much. And this situation would cause even toxic gases to stay on the Earth. Therefore, we can thankfully remark that our Earth has been created in the most convenient size for life.

What, Why, and How?-1

Is tomato a fruit or a vegetable?

There are fleshy or dry seed or seeds in a fruit that we call a kernel. According to this axiom, nourishments such as apricot, peach, grape, bean, tomato, cucumber, etc. are technically fruits. Shortly, all kinds of foods having a kernel are placed in the category of fruits. The rest of them, plant roots such as potato, carrot, turnip, onion, garlic, and plant leaves such as cabbage, lettuce and cauliflower—which is indeed originally a flower—belong to the family of vegetables.

Why do we dab water at
starched clothes before ironing?

When water is dabbed, the starch on the cloth melts and therefore the cloth softens. Dabbed water on the cloth is evaporated after hot iron is applied on the cloth, and the cloth becomes hard and straight again.

What, Why, and How?-1

Why don't funnels sometimes let the liquid flow?

The liquid poured into a funnel which is placed on the rim of a bottle starts to tighten gradually the air inside the bottle. Since the air inside has no place to escape, it is stuck and the pressure of it increases. Then there comes a moment where the air pressure inside the bottle increases up to the level high enough to resist the weight of the liquid inside the funnel. At that time, the flow of liquid in the funnel stops and the liquid is gathered in the funnel. In this situation, it is necessary to raise the funnel up a little bit in order to let the air stuck in the bottle go out. After that, the liquid gathered in the funnel shall start to flow into the bottle again.

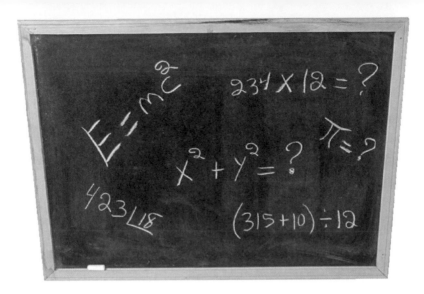

Why does writing on a board with chalk make an irritating sound?

While we are writing on a board with chalk, we press the chalk on the board and move it. During this friction, particles are broken off from the chalk and these particles cling to the board. If this friction between the board and the chalk is less than it should be, the chalk slips and touches to the board many times one after another. As a result, that irritating sound of a scrape is heard.

Why are fog lights generally yellow?

A fog light should have such a feature that it can both pass through the fog and enlighten the front of the vehicle. Red light is the light that is dispersed the lowest level by fog particles and that's why it is the most suitable light that can pass through the fog. However, red light is weak when providing strong lighting that it is necessary for a driver to see both the road and warning lights. The most sensitive light for the human eye is yellow light. In addition, yellow light has almost the same effect as red light in terms of passing through the fog. Since yellow light enables both road visibility and penetrates through the fog, it is used as fog lights.

Why do turtles shed salty tears?

Turtles drink salty water while swimming in the sea and they need to put off extra salt in their bodies. For this reason, when they come to coast for leaving their eggs, they shed salty tears. So, they put out extra salt from glands around their eyes, through the Divine drive, as a sign of absolute mercy and wisdom.

What, Why, and How?-1

How can cats see very well in dark?

There is a special reflective surface on the back part of cat eyes that enables them to see all the coming light at a doubled level. This reflective surface facilitates seeing in the dark for cats. Owing to this special creation, cats move easily in complete darkness at nights.

Sources

› *107 Kimya Öyküsü*, L. Vlasov, D. Trifonov, Ankara: TÜBİTAK, 1998

› *Bilim ve Teknik*

› *Bilim Çocuk*

› *The Fountain*

› *Gündelik Bilmeceler*, Partha Ghose, Dipankar Home, Ankara: TÜBİTAK, 2002

› *Hayvanlar Ansiklopedisi*

› *My Big Question and Answer Book*, London: Kingfisher, 1999

› *National Geographic*

› *Seçilmiş Gezegen*, Aslı Kaplan, İstanbul: Muştu, 2008

› *Sızıntı*

› *Tabiatta Mühendislik*, M. Sami Polatöz, İstanbul: Kaynak, 2003

› *Zafer*

Web Sites

› www.biltek.tubitak.gov.tr

› www.biltek.tubitak.gov.tr/cocuk

› www.fountainmagazine.com

› www.kimyaokulu.com

› www.nix.nasa.gov

› www.nsf.gov

› www.sizinti.com.tr

› www.zaferdergisi.com

What, Why, and How?-1